Victim Slayer

Overcoming Your Past, Embracing Your Future

Victim Slayer

Overcoming Your Past, Embracing Your Future

LATOYA ROBERTS

XULON PRESS

Xulon Press
2301 Lucien Way #415
Maitland, FL 32751
407.339.4217
www.xulonpress.com

© 2019 by LaToya Roberts

All rights reserved solely by the author. The author guarantees all contents are original and do not infringe upon the legal rights of any other person or work. No part of this book may be reproduced in any form without the permission of the author. The views expressed in this book are not necessarily those of the publisher.

Unless otherwise indicated, Scripture quotations taken from the Holy Bible, New International Version (NIV). Copyright © 1973, 1978, 1984, 2011 by Biblica, Inc.™. Used by permission. All rights reserved.

Scripture quotations taken from the Amplified Bible (AMP). Copyright © 1954, 1958, 1962, 1964, 1965, 1987 by The Lockman Foundation. Used by permission. All rights reserved.

Scripture quotations taken from the King James Version (KJV) – *public domain*.

Printed in the United States of America.

ISBN-13: 978-1-54565-828-4

Table of Contents

◊◊◊

Introduction ix
The Victim Slayer xv
Chapter 1: The Pain of a Broken Family
            and Losing Mom 1
Chapter 2: The Abuser Boyfriend 6
Chapter 3: Scared Foster Child 16
Chapter 4: God Wants You to Be Victorious 19
Chapter 5: More on Abuse, Prayer, and Seeking Help 21
Chapter 6: From the Diary of a Broken Young Woman 25
Chapter 7: A Young, Broken, and a Desperate Wife 31
Chapter 8: Enough 34
Chapter 9: Tips on Loving Yourself 35
Chapter 10: The Sting of the Past 39
Chapter 11: Dear Mother of an Abused Child
            (From My Heart to Yours) 43
Chapter 12: Looking Ahead and Dealing
            with the Pain and Loss 45
Chapter 13: Too Much Worry, Not Enough Praying 52
Chapter 14: Road to Recovering It All 55
Chapter 15: Being Free and Staying There 60

Introduction

◇◇◇

There are many people in the Bible whom I could write about in this book; I chose however to focus on just a few faith-filled moments in mighty biblical figures' lives as they are related to my personal story. My prayer is that as you read and identify with some or most of the content, you can see how it relates to these strong figures of the Bible and the Christian faith to inspire and motivate you to learn, grow, and heal as you begin this journey of overcoming a victim mentality. I pray that you will be free of your dark past and unlock all the greatness inside of you that God has purposed for your life.

The Lord Goes before You

As a young boy, David was faced with one of the biggest and heaviest challenges of his life. One day while bringing his brothers lunch to the battlefield, David took on a challenge that everyone feared. He took on the challenge of fighting a giant named Goliath.

David was young and small in stature, but he was strong in faith and had much confidence in God. He knew the same God who allowed him to kill bears and lions (and we know they are animals that will rip any human into shreds and eat them as a meal) would allow David to win this battle. Due to David's faith and dependency on God, God gave him the strength and wisdom he needed to defeat the giant. Not only did he kill the giant, he cut off Goliath's head to make sure he was dead! Whoa! (1 Sam. 17: 12-51).

David's battle was a physical one in which he won through his faith in God. Now I am not saying start throwing rocks at people you have problems with. The battle we are talking about here is a spiritual one, not a physical one (Eph. 6:12). Instead of being Goliath's next victim, God transformed David into the victor!

Deuteronomy 31:8 says, "It is the Lord who goes before you. He will be with you; he will not fail you or abandon you. Do not fear or dismay."

We must spiritually fight our opposer—who is the devil or demons that come in the form of people, your emotions, or situations—to overcome our battles. Trying to work it out in the physical is not always the right option and folding up or giving in is not the solution either. While feeling emotion during a harmful or negative situation is a natural response, staying there too long is detrimental to your physical and spiritual health.

Let's place first things first; In Acts 13:22, Jesus mentions that David is a man after God's own heart. This means David followed the heart of God. God and David had a close enough relationship that he knew God's heart and carried it out. The key to following God's heart is relationship. You should want to follow God's heart because it gives you instant access to what the mind of God is for your life and situation. Having the heart of God will propel you to worship and praise Him and to study the Word so you have the spiritual food needed to equip you with the confidence and power to defeat any situation that comes up in your life.

In following God's heart, you will have a relationship with God. Having a relationship with Him starts with communicating (through prayer) with Him daily. Make sure you mention to God every situation that occurs in your life. Although He knows it already, He wants you to talk to Him about everything. Sharing your experiences with God shows openness to His will and guidance in your life. Along with communicating with Him, you should also begin or increase your Bible time. Studying and reading His word is another very important part to this. When you begin to hear and believe what God says about you, you will begin to get the boldness and courage you need to slay your own giants. David had great boldness; he didn't cry about what he was going through. Instead, he used his faith in God. He took hold of courage, and God gave him the boldness needed to slay the giant standing before him.

Just as we need weapons in a physical fight, we need weapons to fight in the spirit. We need to use our spiritual weapons. Read what Ephesians 6: 10-18 says about spiritual weapons:

> Finally, be strong in the Lord and in his mighty power. Put on the full armor of God so that you can take your stand against the devil's schemes. For our struggle is not against flesh and blood, but against the rulers, against the authorities, against the powers of this dark world and against the spiritual forces of evil in the heavenly realms. Therefore put on the full armor of God, so that when the day of evil comes you may be able to stand your ground, and after you have done everything to stand. Stand firm then, with the belt of truth buckled around your waist. With

the breastplate of righteousness in place, and with your feet fitted with the readiness that comes from the gospel of peace. In addition to all of this, take up the shield of faith, with which you can extinguish all the flaming arrows of the evil one. Take the helmet of salvation and the sword of the spirit which is the word of God...."

If the battle is not against flesh and blood, as we read above, who is it against? The battle is against demons over which Satan has control and they are very real. So if we know the battle is not with physical people, and it's all in the spiritual, we must fight in the Spirit with spiritual weapons. Understand it's not the person who may have done wrong to you, but it is the spirit of Satan who is working through them to hurt you.

1. The belt of truth represents God's truth. Satan fights with lies, and sometimes his lies sound like truth. We have God's truth, and it always wins over lies.
2. The breastplate of righteousness: Satan often attacks our heart, which is the seat of our emotions (that's where are emotions reside), self-worth, and trust. This breastplate protects our heart. He loves us, and He sent His son, Jesus, to die for us.
3. Footwear symbolizes the readiness to spread the gospel. Satan wants us to believe that telling others about Christ is worthless. The foot gear gives us that motivation to continue to proclaim the good news that everyone needs to hear. As you begin to become set free you will want to share what God has done in your life.

4. The shield of faith written about above is needed because we see Satan's attacks in the form of setbacks, insults, and temptations. The shield of faith protects us from these tricks to deceive us; Satan's tricks are his flaming arrows. With the help of God, we can see beyond our circumstances and know the ultimate victory is ours.
5. The helmet of salvation protects and guards our minds from all negativity. All the lies that Satan would use to try to hurt you. Even the battle that goes on within yourself, your emotions. That's all originating from Satan. You are a child of God!
6. The sword of the Spirit is the Word of God. This is the only real weapon of offense on this list of armor. There are times we need to fight back in the spirit against Satan. We need to use the Word. If we do not have the Word in us by reading and studying, it cannot come out, and we will not be able to defeat Satan in this battle and other battles going forward. Satan cannot stand when you know and use the powerful Word of God. It's guaranteed to be effective (Isa. 55:11) and as the Word says, God's word will not return empty (untruth). It will accomplish what I desire and achieve the purpose for which I sent it (come to pass).

You don't have to play a victim of your past. The word "victim" means "harmed, injured, or killed as a result of a crime or event or action." When things happen in our lives, Yes, we do become victims, but we should not remain victims. We must get up, and stay up! The enemy wants us to stay down. The scripture says in John 10:10: "The thief comes only to kill steal and destroy, but, I (Jesus) come that you might have life and that more abundantly." The enemy comes to break you, but Jesus will give you a better life.

Believe me remaining a victim means staying hurt, depressed, on mental health medications, continuing or beginning to consume drugs and alcohol, staying in our sinful behaviors, lying, cheating, manipulation, promiscuity, stealing… The list goes on and on.

Give the sins of your past or present to God and allow this book to speak to your heart, spirit, and your mind. Your mind is the gateway to your heart. That means whatever you think can begin to manifest in your heart.

Satan is the opposite of God; he is the deceiver. I like to refer to him as the trickster because he often tricks us into believing something that is not true. In fact, he is the father of deception. No one can ever lie better than him. He will keep deceiving and manipulating you to think there is no way up. But I am here to tell you, you *can* slay your giant! You *can* slay your victim mentality!

The Victim Slayer

Often times, when we go through things and we feel defeated once we have tried to overcome our obstacles on our own. These obstacles are the giants in our lives.

Is a trauma or abuse from your past holding you back from your future? Are you holding a secret that should have been told? Are you acting out inappropriately? Do you feel that you are at the end of your rope? Do you just feel like everyone is better off without you?

Did someone do something wrong to you? Was someone not there for you like they should have been? Was it a parent or perhaps another loved one?

Maybe you are a parent or a loved one who feels they should have been there for him or her?

Do you find yourself having a pity party again and again, only to feel that no one is listening?

Do you know someone in your life described above?

Well my friend, I am talking to you. You picked up this book because God hears you. He wants you to know that you are not alone. You can make it, and most of all, He loves you! Pick yourself up; pick up your tissue, and wipe away your tears.

I am about to take you on a journey of my past. Join me as I relive past moments, often hurtful moments including the loss of both parents, sexual abuse, physical abuse in marriage, and more that led to low self-esteem and self-worth that repeated in my own child's life. The details of my life are not shared in chronological order but in order of relevance.

Some things may be similar to your situation and may "hit home" for you. It's okay to feel emotion or cry. Just know God is healing you at that very moment. So we will cry together and maybe laugh together. Understand that this will bring healing for you. Do you believe that? We need to deal with the past, in order to walk into your future—your destiny! Too much time has passed. Freedom is waiting for you. Your peace is waiting for you. Your joy will be restored.

I overcame, and you will too.

I wasn't always so strong with conviction and courageous in the Lord as I am now. My life had its struggles and with struggles came fear. Faith saw me through, I believe like me it will see you through….. just believe and be open to your healing process. Let this book be the start for you.

Now it's your time. Let's go!

Chapter 1:
The Pain of a Broken Family and Losing Mom

As far back as I can remember, life was pretty good. I was the youngest of two girls. My mother and father were married, and we lived in a very nice area. My mother was a pediatric nurse, and I remember going to work with her on some occasions. I often heard her say she loved children and her work.

My mother was an easygoing person. I remember being able to go outside to play and invite my friends over for dinner, and it was just fine with her. I noticed that many nights my mother would eat peanut butter and jelly sandwiches and give us something better like meat and rice. Quite often, I would notice my mother miss meals so we could eat. She would just simply tell me she was not hungry. I didn't pay much attention to it as a young child, but now as an adult I realize there was a struggle. She never wanted us to feel or know her struggle. Her love for my older sister and I was real, and she never let her pain show.

My father was also with us at home. He was out of the house a lot, so I remember little of him during that time. I do remember listening to music or the stereo in the living room on weekend mornings. I would dance and dance and enjoy the music, particularly the beats and rhythm. In my eyes I had the perfect family: mom, dad, sister, and me.

But sometimes I would hear my parents argue; it made me feel sad and often torn between them because I loved them both. In the middle of the night my aunt and grandmother came to our house, and my mother, grandmother, and aunt started packing things in black garbage bags. My dad came home shortly after and learned we were leaving. He became upset and a heated argument began. Everyone continued packing clothes, and I noticed my father throwing up in the toilet. I loved him too, so I felt really bad. I asked him if he was okay.

He responded, "Yes," so I asked, "Why are you throwing up?"

He said it was because my mother was going away with us. I wanted to cry; I didn't want to leave my dad. I loved him and couldn't understand why my mother would want to leave him. My five-year-old mind thought my mother was being mean to him. After that I remember being quiet for the rest of the time. I felt sorry for my dad, and I didn't want to leave him. I think this was probably my first heartbreak. What I felt was the best family was actually separating. A part of my heart would stay in Massachusetts, and the other half would be going with me to New Jersey.

We arrived in New Jersey with my mother and sister. One day while in my first grade classroom, I remember being excited about my mother coming home from the hospital. She planned to pick me up from school that day. I was only about six years old then and really didn't know why she was in the hospital. All I knew was that I missed her very much.

She picked me up from school, and on our walk home from school that day, we stopped in the hair salon because my older sister (who was ten years old at the time) was getting her hair done. We walked in and sat down to wait for her stylist to finish. My aunt and mother sat on one bench, and I and my grandmother sat on another. There was much talking in the salon, and the television was on.

My grandmother was talking to my mother, and I really wasn't paying much attention to their conversation until I heard my grandmother call my mom's name, "Sharon! Sharon!" When I looked over, I saw my mother leaning over onto my aunt's shoulder. My grandmother began to scream "CARDIAC ARREST! CARDIAC ARREST!" Someone called 911, and the paramedics came right away.

This time I was stunned and didn't know what to feel. They lowered my mother to the ground and began pounding on her chest. Then I watched as they put oxygen over her face. Then she was taken to the hospital. That day will forever be in my memory.

A few days later, my aunt picked my sister and I up from school and took us to see our mother. I loved my mother and had missed her so much, so I was really excited to see her. It had been hard to be separated from her a second time. My mother never left us except to go to work. See, the day she went into cardiac arrest at the salon was the very day she was released from her first hospital stay, which was a stay that lasted weeks.

When I was told she was coming home from her first hospital visit, I was so excited. I told my teacher my mother was coming home from the hospital, and I told all my friends. She, in fact, came to pick me up from school that day. I remember the feeling of being hugged and kissed by my mother as we made our way to the salon and my sister. We talked as we walked there together.

However, I really wasn't prepared for the condition she would quickly be in.

As I walked into the hospital room, I saw her lying in the bed. She had a tube coming out of her neck, so I was hesitant to walk over to her. She was my mom, though, so I went. She looked at me, but she couldn't talk. She lowered her eyebrows, and her expression seemed to indicate she didn't know my sister and I. That was such a heartbreak. I looked at my aunt and asked her, "Why is Mommy looking at me like that? Does she know me?"

My aunt told me she had amnesia, and she began to explain to me that amnesia is when you lose your memory. I really didn't know how to respond because I couldn't process in my six-year-old mind that my mom would not know who I was anymore.

A few weeks later, I was told by my aunt and grandmother that my mother had passed away from a heart attack. I had so many questions, and at that time no one would really give us answers. All I knew was I loved my mother very much, and she was gone. I was only six years old and didn't understand what death was; I thought she was just asleep. I remember seeing her at her funeral. I was handing out tissues to the people who had come to mourn her. The more I sat on laps and walked around, the more people cried. They knew I did not know what was really happening. My mother was just lying there beautifully; it looked like she was asleep her eyes and mouth were closed. She had on a pink and white dress with ruffles and lace with diamond and pearl earrings and make up with her hair nicely curled.

The reality of no longer having a mother and never seeing her again really didn't come about until my teenage years. Oftentimes, when I was around my friends and they talked about mother and daughter activities like going to the hair or nail salon, mall shopping, chaperoning a school trip, or any activity that moms usually participate in devastated me. It broke my heart. *Why did my mom have to die?*

was the question I began to ask myself. This was the second heartbreak for me, and I was only six years old at the time of her passing.

Often, I would sit on the floor in the corner of my room in the dark crying and screaming at God for taking away my mother. I felt no one would ever understand my pain, and the more my peers talked about their moms, the more it hurt. I became very angry at God. Why did he have to take my mother? I figured all kids should have a mother. I became rebellious after years of carrying this hurt. As you continue to read you will learn as the years passed how I dealt with the loss of my mother; this is a pain no one on this physical earth can understand. Pain can make you do things that cannot help build a successful life. So I made mistakes, and as more trauma happened in my life, I sank deeper into my pain.

Chapter 2:

The Abuser Boyfriend

◊◊◊

At the age of ten years old, I was living at my aunt's home with my sister and my aunt's two sons. My mother had passed away four years earlier, and I was still hurt that she left me. My aunt was very nice to me. I was the youngest of the four of us—her two sons, my sister, and I.

One day we took a ride in the car then we parked the car and got on a bus that drove us to a gaited area. When we got off the bus, my aunt gave her name and the name of the person she was coming to see to the person there, and they called for this person, "City" is what they called him, to come outside. He was escorted outside. I didn't know him, but my aunt did, and she gave him a kiss on the lips. People were outside eating food and playing; it was a BBQ. As the years have passed, I realized it was family day at the prison in which my aunt's boyfriend was incarcerated.

After that day, we went to visit him a few more times but in a more closed setting. It was a corner building where guards were watching. My aunt would send us off to the table next to them, so they could kiss or touch each other secretly. Apparently, that was something all visitors did with the inmates because when I would look around, I saw many were doing it. I didn't really like going on these visits, but I had to go. A few years later, we started visiting him in a house they called a "halfway house," and then he moved in with us.

At first things were awesome; he bought me everything I wanted. I got every teddy bear, every doll… He even slipped me money when no one was around. He became my friend but told me not to tell anyone he was giving me all the extra money and candy and things. I began to trust him, and I felt safe with him.

One day my aunt went out to the store and left me and my two cousins home with him. The three of us were in the living room sitting down watching television. He was in his bedroom, and I heard him call one of the boys to come to his room. He went and came back with popcorn. Then he called me.

I went to his room to get popcorn too, or so I thought. When I arrived, he was sitting on the bed. "Close the door," he said. So I did.

"Do you love me?" he asked.

"Yes" I responded, and he put his hand out to get a hug, so I hugged him.

I started to feel uncomfortable. He laid back so I would end up on top of him. Then he came back up and said, "Pull down your pants."

"No," I said, but he countered, "Do you see that picture on the wall up there? I will break it and tell your aunt you did it."

Now let me explain: The picture was a blow up size portrait of my mother. It was the only large picture my aunt or anyone in my family had of my mother. If he would even mention I broke that picture, I felt my aunt would have beat me. So what does a kid do? I listened and pulled down my pants.

So, his niceness was called grooming. Most abusers use this to gain the trust or friendship of the child to make it easier to begin this abuse and keep it going. As if I didn't have enough hurt and heartbreak in my life—now abuse!

The molestation went on for years, and he threatened to kill me if I told anyone. I was very scared of him but told my aunt anyway when he was not at home because I trusted and loved her. I felt she would not do anything to hurt me because I was her blood; I was her only sister's child. I knew she loved me, and she was considered my second mom. I believed she would protect me. She promised me she would not tell him. I believed her with my whole heart. However, she told him. I felt betrayed, devastated, and feared for my life. I became a sad and very timid child.

Betrayal is a painful emotion that can rip apart our self-confidence and our ability to trust. It will leave you feeling empty inside. Having someone close to you whom you love and trust turn their back on you can break apart even the strongest person. My mother left me a long time ago, and now my aunt whom I viewed as another mom left me, too. That's how I felt in my heart.

My aunt telling on me instead of protecting me just made things worse for me. Now when my aunt was not around, he became not only more sexually abusive but physically and verbally abusive toward me as well. There were many occasions that I wished I was dead. I wanted my mother, but the only one who would love and protect me no longer existed.

I used to write letters to her and would keep them in a shoebox under my bed. In these letters, I told her of all my pain, hoping she would hear me. I would also take her picture, place it in a chair, and talk to it alone, hoping she would hear me. Because I was in pain, I stopped trusting people.

My aunt whom I loved so much told the man who threatened to take my life that I told on him, and then he showed me that at any time he could kill me without having any guilt about it. It left me feeling worthless and alone. I particularly remember one morning while I was sitting at the table eating my breakfast...I didn't want to take my vitamins because I was afraid to swallow pills. He came over to me and with a rough voice said, "You better swallow those now!" When I continued to hesitate, he took the pills, grabbed open my mouth, and forced the vitamins down my throat. I thought I was going to choke to death. He was full of rage, and he hated me so much. Out of fear, no one at the table did anything to help me out. My cousins sat quietly at the table.

But I remember often seeing Grandma pray when she lived with us previously, so while I was alone in my room, I would sometimes repeat some of the things she would say like, "Lord help!" and just cry. I knew he was abusing my older sister as well, but she went to school and reported it and was removed from the home. She was older and had no problem speaking out. When they came to the house to see me, I didn't say anything because I was too afraid, but there were tears in my eyes.

There is more about my escape from this abuse in the next chapter. I was also removed from my aunt's home and after suffering more abuse in foster care, I went to live with my grandmother. More about that later. Here, I'd like to share how my aunt's story continues.

A few years after getting to grandma's house and settling in, I was about fourteen years old then. I learned then that my aunt was in the hospital. Grandma went to visit her a few times, and she let me know her health and prognosis wasn't good.

This is the same aunt whose boyfriend molested me; the one who told him I told her what was happening. While I was hurt and felt betrayed by her, I still loved her. She was my second mother and was the closest I could get to my mom on earth. I wanted to know how she was doing.

The day I was supposed to go visit her with Grandma, I noticed a small bump on my leg. Grandma immediately told me that it looked like chicken pox, and I was not able to go see my aunt that day. I was very disappointed, but I was told that due my aunt's condition, I would make things worse for her if she caught the virus. I understood that. She told me my aunt was sitting up in bed and talking, which we all felt was an improvement from when we first heard of her being there.

About two weeks later, the day I got to actually visit, my aunt no longer could talk. Her condition was rapidly failing. You see, she had HIV and had contracted pneumonia. When I saw her lying in the hospital bed, she was pale and very skinny. She sort-of reminded me of a skeleton. Her eyes looked like they would pop out their sockets, and they were yellow. I didn't even recognize her.

At that very moment, my heart dropped and broke into a million pieces. She was truly not what I expected to see in the hospital bed. I expected to see the beautiful, light skinned, thick and curvy built person I always knew. I was about fourteen years old at the time and didn't know how to take this. She kept staring at me. Then she began trying to speak, grunting, groaning, and trying to clear her throat. I kept rubbing her forehead and told her not to strain herself. No one was in the room, it was just me and her for the moment. She kept clearing her throat and trying to form words, but she couldn't.

Then I thought maybe she was trying to apologize to me for not believing me and telling her boyfriend about what I said. After a few minutes of hearing her try to speak, I told her, "I forgive you; I forgive you." She continued trying to speak and began looking up at the ceiling. I began praying out loud for her. Asking God to forgive her of any sins, give her peace, and let her know for real that I forgave her. Something inside of me nudged me to pray for her; it wasn't easy, and I did not have the words to say.

I wasn't sure if this was the last I would see her alive, but I wanted her to know I loved her, and I forgave her. After praying for her, I noticed her looking up at the ceiling and trying to lift her hands upward over and over a few times. I grew nervous and left the room. Soon after I found out that she passed away. It hurt me, but I remember thinking, *Thank you, God. At least I was able to tell her I forgave her, and I loved her.*

I really didn't know what she was trying to say to me, but the visit with her was a moment of closure for me. I didn't have to go through the rest of my life feeling like my aunt didn't love or care for me. I saw the love and sincere sorrow in her eyes. I believe we connected on her death bed, and I thank God for that.

The loss of a loved one is painful, and the loss of a loved one who resides in your heart daily is even worse. It is truly a hard pill to swallow. The pain I felt when I realized my mother wasn't coming back was unbearable most of the time. Then to now have the one I viewed as a second mother gone too? How was I to go on with life? I had to take one moment at a time, until it was each day at a time…

On Loss of a Loved One

I know the pain of losing your mom or someone else very close to you. If this is you, understand that it may seem like you can't go on. I know the hurt you feel when you are alone at night crying for your loved one; I understand the feeling of anger you experience when you hear someone mention their own mother or loved one. I understand the feeling of sadness that comes when your loved one missed some of the most important moments of your life: the birth of your child, marriage, when you first learned to drive, your prom, high school graduation, college graduation…

Or maybe you haven't lost your mom or loved one in the natural, but they have not been there for you emotionally and physically. They may have been incarcerated or chose another lifestyle, and you weren't included. Maybe you were adopted or were a foster child, and your parents were not involved. Whatever the story may be that is still a loss for you.

God says He has seen every tear that fell from your eyes. You know that time when you cried so much you fell asleep? Well, He was there crying with you and holding you and rocked you to sleep. He was and is always with you.

What about that time you took a lot of pills at one time to end it all and you went to sleep and woke up the next day?

What about the time you went for the knife to slit your wrist, and it didn't cut? Or when someone came at the right time and stopped you?

What about when you were at some place you weren't supposed to be, but because of your pain, you were there. The trigger was pulled and the bullet was released and just grazed your head, or did it completely miss you? You have a purpose, a God-given purpose.

God has more for you in life than what you have experienced; He has more for you than what you are currently going through. He sees and hears all things.

Understand that while you were going through your trauma, He was there and kept things from getting much worse for you. You may believe it couldn't have been worse and didn't feel Him there. It's good you say that, and I completely understand. But when I realized what could have happened to me; I knew God was there! You will understand more when you continue to read because I will tell you in a later chapter how God covered me, even when I was a little girl and didn't know how to pray or call on Him.

You see, when you hurt God also hurts. That's because at one time He was fully God and fully man. When He walked this earth in a human body over two thousand years ago, He did that for you and me. He did that so He could experience pain and loss and all the emotions we feel. So I am not encouraging you to reach out to a God who has never felt or had personal experiences. He has experienced loss as well, and He can walk this season out with you. At this very moment, let God touch your heart wherever you are. Forgive your abuser; forgive that family member who didn't believe you or didn't want you to speak out. Most of all, forgive yourself! Let God speak to you. Forgiveness is necessary for you to grow and heal. You owe it to yourself.

Food for thought:

When you do not forgive you begin to bottle up pain, bitterness, and anger that can negatively affect your health. Remaining in an emotional state of anger puts you into a flight or fight mode. Fight or flight is a quick stress response that literally takes your blood pressure from normal to extremely high. It can also enable you to do things you normally wouldn't be able to do under normal circumstances.

You may think, *Hey that's not a bad idea*, but it truly is very bad because it puts extreme stress on your body in a very short period of time. The physiological changes can damage you inside if you remain in that state, and unforgiveness keeps you there. Some changes that can occur in your body are heart rate changes; it can also increase the risk of depression, heart disease, and diabetes.

I learned that keeping that person locked up in your mind and heart keeps you burdened with pain and anger while the person who harmed you is not really thinking much about your or the situation itself. Most of the time they don't even know you are still upset with them. Forgiving the one who hurt you frees you. The consequences of unforgiveness are not worth the struggle and stress you endure over someone who has done you wrong. When you forgive, you free yourself—mind, body, and spirit.

As a young girl, I forgave. I wanted to feel better; I didn't want the hurt my aunt caused me to keep me down, so I forgave her.

Even though my aunt didn't respond well when I shared the abuse her boyfriend was inflicting on me, she was still my aunt and like my second mom; I loved her. Her passing was a great loss for me. I had to forgive her, so I could begin to heal from my trauma and hurt. She was still my aunt, and I know she loved me.

In understanding my loss, I had to understand that God is in control of everything; He does what He wants and always knows the best decision for every situation. No matter how your loved one died, you really don't know how their future would have turned out if they had lived longer, but God knows.

Each person who comes into the world has a death day and time, and how each person's death will occur is already known by God. There is nothing anyone can do to stop it, just as there is nothing anyone can do to bring a loved one back.

You who remain alive have to find a way to eventually move on for yourself and for your loved one. It is assumed that no one's loved one would want to see your life going downhill because they are no longer here. They are your loved one for a reason. Not only do you love them, but they love you too.

So remember and enjoy your fond memories, and ask God to give you strength and comfort and move on! You are no longer a victim of loss but a victor of life! Yes, Lord! God can, if you allow Him to, heal your heart of the pain. The memories will be forever engrained in your memory and heart, but the sting of your loss can become less.

There is no pain that God can not heal. It doesn't happen overnight but over time.

Chapter 3:

Scared Foster Child

◊◊◊

Shortly after my sister reported my aunt's boyfriend and was taken away, I was called from class to the school office. When I arrived, the principal greeted me and said someone was in the back room to see me. I really didn't know what was going on and was afraid that it was him, my aunt's boyfriend, coming to pick me up early.

When I walked into the room, I realized it was the social worker who came to the house a few days before. She asked me a few questions, and I told her about how happy I was about being able to spend time with my aunt, especially because I felt she did not love me anymore after I told her what happened to me—after I told her what her boyfriend did to me. I wasn't sure if she thought I was just trying to accuse him of something that wasn't true. But we made a cake together; I was happy to get that time and attention. I was the youngest child in the house, and she always favored me more because I was the baby of the house. I told the social worker how happy I was and how excited I was to lick the batter off of the spoon and enjoyed pouring the colorful sprinkles on top.

The lady told me she felt she should come to the school and talk with me because she saw my "big bright eyes fill with tears" when she visited my aunt's house. She knew it was more than just the cake. She was right; I was being abused but I was afraid to tell anyone. She apparently knew what questions to ask me. She saw my body language and watched my responses, and I am sure there were many indicators that led her to her judgement that my aunt's home was not a good environment for me.

I never went back to the place I had known as home from the age of six, when my mother passed away, to that day, at twelve years old, when I was called to the school office. My mother asked my aunt to raise my sister and me while she was on her sick bed. I was taken to foster care immediately from school that afternoon.

The foster home I was taken to was the same one in which my sister was living. I was happy to be with my sister. It wasn't my aunt's home, but I was glad my sister and I were together. While it was bad at my aunt's house, I missed the familiarity of home and had mixed emotions about not being there. I missed my aunt and cousins, but I knew in the foster home things would be better for me because the bad guy wasn't there.

How much better remained the question. Shortly after the door closed behind the social worker, I realized I would be living in a cold, dark basement with my sister and one other foster child. We slept on metal beds with thin mattresses. It was winter, so we had electric blankets to keep us warm while we slept. We had a lamp to see with during the day, but it was a very dark and scary place down there at night.

During meals, we ate upstairs after the family finished, and once we were done, we were responsible for washing dishes and cleaning the kitchen before heading back to the basement. We played board games downstairs, did one another's hair, and we would sometimes sneak to watch television on the office television downstairs when no one was around in the foster dad's office.

I don't remember much about the foster dad, but I do remember him being a creepy man who told us he was a doctor of "women's private parts." One night I was awakened in my sleep by him examining me with a flashlight in my private area. He thought I was asleep, but I was not. I was afraid to let him know I was awake or scream because I was scared of what he might do to me. So that morning I told his wife, but she didn't believe me and wanted me removed from her home right away.

That same morning I talked to my sister who says she saw him, and my sister had a physical altercation with the foster mother about it and was taken to another home that morning. I never asked the other girl if it happened to her as well. I only talked to my sister. I was scared and didn't want anyone else to know what happened.

That same evening, while looking out the window, I saw my grandmother walking up to the porch to pick me up and take me home with her to her house. I felt like she had come to rescue me. In my eyes, she was my savior. Still today when I remember that moment, it brings a warm feeling. It was a happy moment for me: I finally felt loved. One cannot imagine how happy and relieved I was.

Chapter 4:

God Wants You to Be Victorious

Let's talk a little. God wants to bring healing to you

right at this very moment, and if you are open, you can receive it. You may have gone through the loss of a loved one or sexual abuse like myself or abuse in another form, but hear this: God can fix it.

I know from experience that abuse victims carry excruciating pain within; however, I also know that God knows your pain. If you are at the point of giving up on life, don't. Your pain is only temporary; it's not permanent. God is here for you and wants you to be healed. Don't end your life. Instead cast your cares on your heavenly Father. He can carry all your burdens because He is the burden bearer. 1 Peter 5:7 says, "Cast all your cares on him because he cares for you." Isn't it good to know that God is willing to carry your burdens and stress for you? That's how much He loves you. Who do you know that can honestly say to you, "Don't worry about anything; let me deal with it for you?" I think your answer would be, "No one can or is even willing to do that, but God can and He will. So just give him what he wants. He wants to handle all your problems big and small.

The Bible also says in Luke 1:37, "For with God nothing shall be impossible." (I strongly encourage you to remember this verse.)

God wants you to be free because that gives you victory over the enemy! The enemy wants you to be bound up and confused and remain brokenhearted. God wants you free, and He says He can fix it. He will if you let Him.

God can heal you and restore you, He is the master and you are His masterpiece. You only need to let Him into your heart and mind. He will never leave you. Even when it seems like He's not there, He is. He has heard your cry!

Wont you pray with me?

Father, we come to You today asking You to heal my sister's/ brother's heart today. Heal his or her mind Lord God, and take away all the pain, the hurt of the trauma, the abuse, he or she has endured. Father, I know You have a purpose for the life of my sister or brother, but Lord we know Your purpose cannot be completely fulfilled if they are not completely healed, if they are not made whole. So Father, make them whole again, in Jesus's name we pray. AMEN!

Chapter 5:

More on Abuse, Prayer, and Seeking Help

A lot of times we, the abused, fail to tell anyone because

we are afraid. The fear is for a number of reasons, but the main one is because the abuser threatened in some way. The threat is usually to kill or harm you or your close family member. My advice is to tell someone you trust; get help!

I thank God I was bold enough to tell my aunt, even though she told my abuser. God covered and protected me, so "City" did not end my life. He didn't break the picture of my mother either.

God protects and covers us even when we don't know He's there. He loves us that much. The situation you are in or endured in the past, could be or could have been much worse. Let's thank God that it isn't/wasn't!

My molester told me he would sleep with me for real when I turned thirteen. I left the house at twelve. He was HIV positive. This was GOD'S PROTECTION! God was there all the time, even when I didn't know Him. God was there; He loved me and kept me safe and protected because He has a purpose for my life. God has a purpose for your life. That's why you are still here. Remember that!

Usually the abuser's threat to keep you from telling anyone about the abuse is to deceive or trick you to keep you silent, so the abuse can continue, and he or she will not be caught. Always remember this: Satan is a deceiver (Revelation 12:9)

Victims of abuse or trauma tend to feel alone or depressed and often exhibit behaviors or lifestyles that may not be what God has ordained for their lives.

If you are an abuse victim, you may make decisions that take you off of a godly course for a healthy life. You may enter wrong relationships. Trying to fill a void, you dive into pre-marital sex, marry the wrong partner, abuse drugs or alcohol… The list of behaviors opposed to God's blueprint of how life should be lived seems endless. Your life appears to be all over the place.

Sometimes the abused one becomes the abuser. If you sit down to talk with people who have abused people sexually, you find out that many of them have been abused themselves and have not received proper help.

Stop right here: If this is you, lift your hands, let's bind up the hand of the enemy right now in prayer:

> *We command the spirit of perversion to leave this individual right now. The blood of Jesus is against any unclean spirit! Leave now in Jesus's mighty name—NOW!*

Please go to your pastor or church leader, confess and seek counseling, so you can remain free in Jesus's name. There is a ministry that will be birthed out of you. If you don't go to church, let me encourage you to find a good place of worship; it's good to be around other sisters and brothers who are seeking God together. You need God in your life to break up those things that were not given to you by Him.

Many mistakes I mentioned are not made only by people who have endured the traumas I mentioned in this book. Anyone can partake in these actions, but I do find a lot of these reactions are the direct result of some sort of sexual trauma the person has endured.

In fact, I find that many people have endured this awful trauma but for some reason have remained silent or family chose to keep it silent and not deal with the problem at hand. In reading different articles about this issue, I know the numbers are not accurate. Because it only factors in the cases that were told. No one really knows how many unspoken cases of people walking around, also cases of people who have taken it to the grave with them in death the secret dies with them. It doesn't help anyone, it in fact allows the next person to suffer the trauma.

This is not something that has happened to me or you only; it happens to many children, teenagers, and adults. Abuse also affects the way victims view themselves and others is different. A child victim, for example, is more sensitive and possibly more open to inappropriate behavior for their age, which happens because they usually develop low self-esteem, feel worthless, and develop an abnormal or distorted view of sex and love. They can become promiscuous sometimes or can withdraw or become suicidal.

Here is an example of how two nine-year-old girls, one a victim of sexual abuse and the other not, would likely react to a boy they like:

The molested girl likes this thirteen-year-old boy and likes to do inappropriate things with him. The unmolested nine-year-old thinks the same boy is cute but that sexual encounters are gross.

Do you get it? The girls like the same boy, but the girl who was molested is more open to viewing love and acceptance differently. She may feel that in order to be liked or accepted, she needs to act in an inappropriate way. She needs to be watched or guided by her parents or guardian because of what she has endured to keep her safe.

The abused girl doesn't really want to act out wrongly, but because she has already seen sexual behavior or experienced it in physical form, she has developed a distorted view, and has been opened up to a world she is not ready to experience. She is a child, and should have been playing with her dolls or latest games and trying to learn how to braid hair. Instead, she was taken to a dark place where her childhood was taken away.

Sexual intercourse is designed by God for two consenting adults: biblically speaking, husband and wife!

Therefore, rest assured God will deal with the perpetrator in His own time and in His own way. Don't worry anymore if he or she was never exposed or even punished by any human on earth. Your heavenly father sees all and will deal with them! Let that go, and move on. Move forward for yourself, your marriage, your children, and your loved ones: be free in Jesus's name!

You say, "It's not that easy…" No; it is not that easy, but if you begin and continue to speak it in your mind, it will eventually flow into your spirit, and you will begin to feel it. Nope, it doesn't happen overnight, but it can be done.

How do I know?

Because I got through it. God fought the battle for me. My abuser never went back to jail, and I was not believed by my loved ones at the time. However, he is no longer on this earth due to AIDS. God most certainly protected me from contracting the disease. No; I am not rejoicing that he is dead; however, I do know he has gone on to be judged by God. I am at peace knowing that.

Chapter 6:

From the Diary of a Broken Young Woman

Abuse victims often have a rough lives, and mine is no exception. We begin to make irresponsible decisions that cause our life to crumble.

It is not uncommon for us to end up with children out of wedlock or experience a failed marriage because we are looking to fill a void. Something precious was taken from us in our childhoods, and we want to be happy finally. So we, with our distorted view of life gained through abuse and low self-esteem, run to that man who tells us we are cute and fine. Our body looks right, and we allow him to use us, even knowing he is not committed to us or the relationship. The abused person begins to seek happiness and love in other people. They view love in an unhealthy, warped way. They take something or a situation that can potentially harm them and view it as love and what love really is when in fact this it is so far from the truth. Love does not hurt; love is not ANY type of abuse.

Here's how it was going into adulthood…

I came to live with my grandmother at the age twelve or thirteen. Living there included going to church every Sunday, and later almost every day. I knew I wasn't supposed to indulge in premarital sex, but I felt like I was already tainted. In those times, no one really talked about abuse and such. It happened, and that was it. So you kept the hurt inside and snuck around with boys.

I met a young man at the church I attended. He and I "went together" for many years. It started around the age of twelve, fresh after the molestation, and right after I arrived at my grandmother's house. Me, the broken young lady, became sexually involved with him at around the age of fifteen. We remained "friendly" all the way through middle school, high school, and then during my freshman year in college.

I decided to live on campus because I had nowhere else to stay. At the age of seventeen, my grandmother kicked me out of her house because I didn't listen and obey the rules set for me. I felt I knew more than her. I was sneaking out with friends, having sex, and I didn't care. I believed I was mature enough to make decisions for myself without any help. Due to past trauma and hurt, I couldn't trust. I didn't even trust my grandmother. Whatever she or anyone else (like her friends) said could not convince me I was wrong. I believed I was right and knew all the answers I needed to know. So I continued in a relationship with this young man, even though my grandmother did not like him or approve. I honestly felt that I was grown up in a young girl's body. Hey! I was having sexual encounters as an adult would. However, this young man wasn't always the nicest to me; he treated me poorly most of the time, but nothing he did or said could change my mind about him. So because I persisted in my own belief and was not willing to listen to my grandmother and end the relationship, I was kicked out of my home.

Yes, I was willing to be homeless just to be with him. I couldn't live with him though because he was only seventeen and living with his parents. My grandmother was and "old school," no nonsense type of person. She was tiny in stature, no more than 5 feet 3 inches tall, but she was very strict. I believe her advanced age and how she was raised in the south caused us to disagree on a lot of things. I was only a teenager, and she was in her sixties when I came to live with her. We had a huge age gap, so there was always difficulty expressing my opinions or feelings, and as a result, I never felt she loved me during this time. She never hugged me, or even held me, or told me she loved me. So her putting me out of the house was really confirmation in my mind that she did not love or care for me. A few weeks before this happened, my grandmother told me a lady wanted to meet me.

My grandmother told me my mother's childhood friend looked my mother up in the yellow pages (this was a book that you could look up a person to find their address and phone number, something like Google or maybe Facebook today), and while the lady could not find my mother because she was deceased, she found my grandmother and called looking for my mother. When my grandmother told her my mother had passed but her daughter was living with her, the lady was interested in meeting me. We didn't really get to meet, but when I was kicked out, it was to go live with the lady. I didn't know her, but she was nice. She had a beautiful apartment, and I lived with her there during my last few months of high school.

I was happy there and was able to do anything I wanted. She was never home, so I had the apartment literally to myself, which was perfect. My boyfriend could come over whenever he wanted. I felt my life was set, life was easy, at that time. The lady would call and check up on me and stop by home every week to bring me large amounts of cash for food and whatever I needed and wanted.

This arrangement came to an end soon after I graduated high school, so I decided to live on campus in college. I definitely wasn't going back to grandma's house; I still did not want to listen and follow her rules. Living on campus would still give me the freedom to do what I wanted. So that's what I did. I moved onto campus.

My boyfriend, though, decided he wanted to break up. He wanted to be free to date other people, while I still wanted to remain in a relationship with him. It was clear he didn't want to be serious, but I still tried to make it happen.

Just as broken, confused young ladies will do, I still slept with him on a regular basis. One day, while living on campus, I skipped my birth control and invited him over to have sex, and I got pregnant. He didn't want to be a dad, but I wanted to be a happy family—exactly what I saw others have.

He told me to have an abortion, but I refused. I wanted someone to love me. I didn't really know much about parenthood. He told me he wasn't ready, I just wanted to desperately start that "good life." I wanted to fill the void that I should have received from childhood. I was looking for the things in life that help you become emotionally happy and stable. It wasn't easy to walk around with no one to care for me. The only one who would ever love me for real was my mom, and she was gone. I didn't have my aunt, and my grandmother was strict, and I thought she was mean to me. Eight months into the pregnancy, the school told me I had to move off campus because I was a liability living there while so far along in my pregnancy.

I remember at around five months pregnant, I called my grandmother and invited her out for lunch. We talked and ate, and that is when I revealed to her I was pregnant. I also told her that day how I appreciated what she had done for me, and I apologized to her for being rebellious. I shared that I realized my life was going to be complicated with a child. She was very upset, and, I am sure, hurt. I asked her to forgive me and asked if we could try to move on.

So when the school asked me to leave from living on campus, my grandmother asked her friend, who was my sister's foster mother, if I could stay there during the last weeks of pregnancy and remain there with the baby after it arrived. She said yes, so I moved in with her and had my own room. My sister was already grown and had moved out the house. We are four years apart in age, so she was about twenty-three or twenty-four years old. She already had a son and was living with the father and his family.

I had my beautiful baby girl at twenty years old; it wasn't easy. She didn't sleep well at night. She was born with premature swallowing reflexes, so after she had her milk bottle, if she was not burped like twenty times, it would come back up. If she was lying down, it would choke her. At night, being in the crib was too risky for her, so she had to lay in bed with me to sleep. I was often awakened by her kicks and realized she was choking. She was light skinned, so her face turned red.

When she was an infant, during the day, and sometimes at night, I would have to leave her sitting up in her car seat. It was very stressful. I worked a full-time job then and was taking college classes too. I had the baby hoping it would keep my ex-boyfriend around, but it didn't. I struggled to take care of her both emotionally and financially.

He would come visit her and feed her, but he had to get home and left. As the years went on, I completely dropped out of school and got my own apartment. The reality of being a mom had set in. I felt alone and had no one to rely on for support. Grandma was old school, which means if you have a baby before you finish school, you raise it alone.

The baby held him around sometimes, and I was okay with that. Again, I was a broken young lady. A couple of years later I got pregnant again by the same guy; this time he decided to marry me. I don't think it was because he loved me but because he felt the pressure of needing to do the right thing. He knew I wouldn't abort this child either. I wanted people to love me and felt at least children would never stop loving me because I would never stop loving them. It also was a start to me gaining family. Along with that, I felt that I would be forever connected to this person, my children's father, no matter what happens. I figured the children would make him love me, in case he wasn't sure. I figured we would be happy. My babies were already employed even as a seed in my belly. The job was to keep their dad and I together, make us happy, and to connect me to a family.

I knew he was out there with other women, but I wasn't healed. I was so unhappy with myself and I felt no one would ever want me. We had such a long history together, and we had already started a family. After enduring so many losses and trauma, I just wanted to be normal and have a normal life for once.

We got married; I knew it felt wrong, but I still wanted it. He told me he changed, that he got baptized, so I said yes. One thing I knew was that I wanted to be married to someone who loved God. My grandmother kept me in church constantly, so I grew to love God and learned of His goodness. I always loved God in my heart.

Chapter 7:

A Young, Broken, and a Desperate Wife

◇◇◇

Life seemed okay for the first few months after our wedding, but then he started leaving the house and staying out late at parties without me. He started receiving secret phone calls late at night while at home in bed, and when I asked about the calls or wanted to check his phone, he would respond in a mean way, even sometimes in rage. So I knew he was cheating again. Then he became physically abusive toward me. I had to physically defend myself, and I fought back using objects in my home. I remember throwing dishes and flinging cable wires, which cut him in the palm of his hand. He bled, and he had to go to the emergency room. I myself have been hit with irons and pots over my head as well.

Things got out of hand. I still loved him, though, and would beg him to come back to the house. Sometimes when he attempted to walk out the door, I would get on the floor and grab hold of his foot or lower leg. He would drag me with his leg because I didn't want to let go. All the while I was screaming and crying, begging him to just come back.

Why do you think I did that? I had no self-worth. It was taken from me when I was a little girl. I was broken and craved love so much that I dealt with whatever was handed me. That means I was told off and humiliated in front of our kids, was physically hit, and even took it when he forced himself on me sexually (even though I knew he was just with another woman). I hated the feeling but dealt with it to have the feeling of being loved—even though it was only an illusion of love.

One day in a heated conversation, I asked him what could I do to keep him from cheating, what would keep him home and happy. He told me to give him a son and name the baby after him. So I got pregnant again—baby number three! This time it was a boy, and I named him after him just as he asked. I just knew things would be better because I gave him exactly what he asked for. But did he stay home? Did he change? Not really. Both the cheating and the abusive behavior continued. It was a toxic relationship.

Reader Note: Having a baby will not keep a man in a committed and faithful relationship if he doesn't want to. It can, in fact, make things a lot worse in the long run.

Everything about our household was dysfunctional: our marriage was dysfunctional, and the dramatic events played out in front of our precious little children. They didn't deserve that, but they were always watching. When I thought they were asleep, they really weren't. The yelling, screaming, crying, hitting, beating... They saw it all.

One morning my little son, I don't remember his age, but he was very small, so he was most likely nearly three years old, revealed to me how our behavior was affecting him and all my children. (Their father and I were separated at that time.) I was in the kitchen making his lunch for school while he was in the living room with his sister.

He was playing, and I clearly heard him say, "When I grow up I am going to have a kid with the mother and not give a care about her."

My daughter, who was around four and a half years old, came running into the kitchen and asked, "Mom, did you hear what he said?"

"Yes," I replied. At that point, all I could do was cry in great sadness.

When you think your children are not listening, they are. When you think they don't know what's going on, they do. They may not speak or know how to express it, but their little minds are analyzing and putting things together.

Here's my advice: do not do or say anything in front of children that does not show love toward one another. Any arguments or raising of voices should not be done in the presence of children.

After all this, I got tired and fed up, and guess what I did?

You guessed it: I left!

Chapter 8:
Enough
◊◊◊

I had had enough and made my final decision. I had lingered, hoping things would work out. I was a product of a broken home myself and didn't want the same for my kids, but it was happening. The divorce needed to happen though. I had to face the fact that I made the wrong decision for my children. I should have waited on God to bring the right person into my life, but because of all that I had gone through, God wasn't moving as fast as I wanted him to. I was a broken girl, and because I was so desperate to have a normal life, I made a wrong choice. It took me many years after the divorce to realize that and to forgive myself and finally to forgive him. Because my children's abnormal behavior reminded me of him and how the dysfunction hurt them early in their lives, I carried the guilt, shame, and weight of what I had chosen for our lives daily. Depression settled deep within me, along with the anxiety and fear of moving forward, but somehow I got the strength to get up and go. I just kept thinking of my kids and what my son said. I knew I would be crushed if he grew up and did to his future wife what his father had done to me.

Chapter 9:
Tips on Loving Yourself
◊◊◊

I had to start loving myself, and that was not easy. After all that I had done, and all the hurt I had caused myself and my children, how could I love myself? As far as I saw, I was a screw up. I hated the image of myself in the mirror. Not only was I unhappy with myself as a person, I also didn't like my outer appearance. I didn't think I was pretty. I had very low self-esteem; a lot of that came from my childhood, but also from going through an abusive relationship, enduring infidelity for many years, and then divorce. These can all break you down and cause your self-esteem to hit the bottom. Divorce is another topic, but it can make you feel like a part of you has died, because it has. This is true even for the person who initiates the divorce process. So, my Toxic marriage on top of the pain and trauma from my early childhood was a very dangerous combination.

In dealing with the current situation, I understood that if I started to love myself, I could do better for my children, myself, and others around me. Grandma always told me, "If you don't love yourself, how can you expect anyone else to?" So I started reading inspirational books that talked about self-love and learning how to love yourself.

If you cannot love yourself, it is hard to see your value and you will always see yourself as less than. So loving yourself is extremely important. Just as it is important to invite God into your life and situation, it is also important to begin the process of healing from the inside out.

It starts with you. When you invite God into your life, He is the only one who can show you love. God is love, so when you think of God, you think of love. He thought of you so much that He sent His son to die on a cross for you. I don't know about you, but I would think twice if someone wanted me to give up my child and ultimately experience a horrible death just for someone else to have a better life. That has to be the most selfless and ultimate love someone can feel for another.

God did that for you and me (John 3:16). If He could do that for me, I know I am special to Him, and I am a special person. So if I am special to Him, why can't I be special to myself? Maybe, I thought, if I start feeling special and loving myself, my children will never have to feel what I felt. To this day, I never want my children to ever go through what I have or to have low self-esteem. It's a very bad feeling and not easy to rise from. It takes work.

When you look in the mirror what do you see? Do you like what you see?

I want you to look yourself in the mirror each day and tell yourself: I am beautiful; I am special; and I am loved. God loves me, and God is love. I am awesomely and wonderfully made (Psalm 139:14-16).

Low self-esteem is not something you are born with. I believe we are born with love already in our DNA since we were created in and through love. The love flows naturally, When we experience negative things in life, that natural love, self-love chips away…

Love the person who stares back at you in the mirror. There can never be another you; God made you special and unique, and when He completed His work in creating you, detailing every feature about you, and stepped back and looked at you in satisfaction, He called you (His creation) awesome and wonderful!

Dear Reader:

No one really knows what you are going through except you and God. You should always make sure to care for yourself and ask God for protection, wisdom and guidance. You should never stay in a dangerous and unhealthy environment to please your friends or family. Otherwise, your loved ones may be viewing you from a casket or visiting you in a padded room. Or not even that, you may be walking around hurting people and damaging more people—like your children and family—because of your pain.

Grab your life and self-worth back in Jesus's name! You are very special to God, and He never said to stay in an unhealthy, abusive knock-down, drag-you-on-the-floor, cheat-on-you marriage. God wants you to be happy. No; He absolutely doesn't say run when things get tough. That's another topic.

I am not encouraging anyone to leave their marriage; marriage takes time, love, and a lot of patience to work. Having a successful marriage requires both persons to keep God as the focus, and both must be willing to work at the relationship. If both are committed to God and each other, marriage will work. This is the key!

Marriage is a beautiful thing and is honored by God. However, there are extremely ungodly situations like my own was, and I say by all means: RUN! RUN, in the name of JESUS! I know firsthand what a toxic situation can do to you.

There are too many people today locked in bondage who need to be free. So I want to pray for you: my sister if you are in an abusive marriage, wherever you are, please lift your hands, and just pray this simple prayer with me from your heart:

> *Lord, I need You to today. Forgive me of all my sins. I need You to free me from this bondage I am in. Free me from the physical bondage of this toxic relationship. Lord I ask that You have Your way. Bring peace and comfort. Father, take away my fear and anxiety and give me strength and clarity to make clear decisions. I also ask You for the courage and boldness I need to make the right decision for myself and my family. In Jesus's name. AMEN!*

I declare freedom in every aspect over Your life in Jesus's name!

I lost a lot of so-called friends. I have been betrayed, talked about, and scandalized, and it's okay.

Let them talk. You continue to love yourself.

Remember, no one can live your life. No one sees what happens behind closed doors. People can talk and give their advice and suggestions, but at the end of the day, you need to make the decision. If your decision makes people talk negatively about you, let them talk. God has your back! As long as you have spoken to God about your decision and asked Him to guide you, trust me, He will do so.

Disclaimer: The statements made above is for the one who is actively in a toxic relationship and need out. This is simply confirmation for you. You know who you are…

Chapter 10:
The Sting of the Past
◊◊◊

Fast forward to a couple years after my divorce. This time I decided to wait on God, and He blessed me with an amazing man in my life who accepted my three children. We met at work when we were teenagers, but soon after meeting him, I left the job, and we lost touch. After about ten or eleven years passed, we bumped into each other, again while I was at work, on a different job, and we began to develop a friendship. A few years after my divorce, we decided we wanted something more than friendship, and we joined together in holy matrimony and were blessed with a child together.

As my ex-husband and I moved on, I didn't want to be the bitter ex, so I initiated visitations with his three children. They visited their biological father regularly, and I started noticing that my oldest daughter began acting abnormally for her age. Of course, I would know the behaviors associated with sexual abuse, because it happened to me. After I investigated, I found out my daughter had been the victim of molestation. It happened at her father's home at the time. The abuser was her uncle, her dad's half-brother.

This abuse started around the time of the legal separation from the father of my children. The children went with their father after school, and the abuse happened at that time. I didn't find out until my divorce paperwork was being finalized. Here I am thinking, *Lord, I came out of this horrible situation and life is good, and now I get a sting like this to remind me of the awful mistake I made of getting entangled with this guy? Could this be punishment? Why me? I can't take this?*

The enemy loves to bring you back to your past when he sees you are moving forward. His job is to always, in some way, sabotage your life and destroy you. If he can keep you down and depressed and doubting God, then he is happy.

Finding out my daughter was molested brought back old hurt for me. I was dragged twenty steps back emotionally. I was angry and hurt and bitter, and I really had to pray. I had to get to know God for real because I knew that was the only way I would make it through this new hurt. I felt that God was the only choice.

It was extremely tough, so some days I couldn't even pray. I didn't feel comfortable confiding in anyone in great detail. I felt that the people that I did tell, didn't take the situation seriously, and I thought they couldn't really feel my pain and understand what I was going through. My current husband could only grieve with me, and my relationship with my father was not strong.

We had lost many years, so the bond we had when I was a child remained the same as it was in childhood. So as an adult I was disconnected from him and felt he just wouldn't understand. I also didn't want to burden him with my issues. At that time, he was already remarried and had his own life.

At the very beginning, while the wound was fresh and deep, I wasn't close enough to anyone with whom I could share with that I felt wouldn't judge me. My daughter's father seemed to be focused around his own life, he couldn't see the pain his daughter was going through. All I knew to do was get help for my daughter. The first step was to call the police and take this matter to the fullest of law, which I did. Justice was granted. I had my daughter in outpatient counselling as support for her. I felt alone; the family on her father's side remained silent.

But I knew God was walking by my side the whole time, and He never left my side. If he had, I would have lost my mind. Without Him, I could have never watched my daughter at age eleven describe on the witness stand what her twenty-one year old molester did to her and not break down and cry in front of her. I had to be strong for her. If I cried, she would have felt bad and cried, and I did not want that, so I had to make her feel comfortable enough to speak. They wanted me out of the room, but I wanted to be in the room as she spoke to the judge. As she described the events that happened to her, I was hearing the clear description for the first time. It took all of God's strength for me to sit through that and not crack a tear or raise a fist in anger or rage toward anyone who looked like my daughter's molester in that courtroom. I was shattered and torn inside, but on the outside that day, I knew I had to have strength and be strong for my daughter.

Weeks passed, and then my daughter began acting out at home. From running away and the police bringing her back home to trying to slit her wrists in front of her younger siblings to displaying inappropriate behavior with boys, it was clear she was hurting. I had her in outpatient counseling, but she had to go inpatient. I missed so many days at work; thank God I didn't lose my job.

Many times I wondered how my husband didn't walk away because the cops were at my house on a weekly basis, and we lived in a quiet, upscale neighborhood. I felt like I was in a whirlwind; my life turned into hell. My daughter was very difficult to handle. This is when I had to really begin crying out to God. I was desperate; my daughter, if God did not turn her around, had a future that was exact opposite of what a mother would want for her child. She was heading down the road of sex, drugs, and alcohol. I wanted so much for her; I wanted her to have better than me. I knew it wasn't going to be easy, but I wanted to be there for my daughter because I didn't want her to feel what I felt as a child.

I still didn't lose hope, and I kept my faith in God. I prayed some days and was weak and could not pray on other days. But God gave me the strength to make it through. I believe He knew the days I didn't have the strength to pray, and He gave me the strength I needed anyway. After all, I am here writing this book for you as an overcomer! While I was going through this I could not see my way through it all, but it all makes sense now. I went through it for you and am so glad I did it.

Even as I write these words, I declare strength to you! You can go through it! You are equipped, and God has given you everything you need to do, so just trust Him. Rest in knowing that He has your back. I know it feels rough and tough; I know you feel like ending it all... but God! He will never let you down. Stop and take a deep breath and slowly let it out; everything is okay. Trust God; He destroys mountains.

While my older daughter was in counseling, I started the two younger children in counseling as well because one of them was having nightmares about the abuse they saw me endure.

Chapter 11:

Dear Mother of an Abused Child (From My Heart to Yours):

I know there is a lot of things running through your mind, and that's okay. Your heart is broken, and I think that is a natural response for you to feel. Your child has been through a lot, and you need to be there for them. Show them love! They need a whole lot of it. Understand that it's not your child's fault. He or she was threatened and lied to.

Right now your child feels powerless and helpless. They may feel they caused this whole thing. They feel fear of being hurt, guilt or shame, Their self-esteem is low. Even if they are acting tough and rebellious, know that's what they are really feeling. Remember, hurt people hurt others almost always in some way. They are acting from a place of pain and desiring love. Hurting people often don't love themselves enough, so they look for love and approval from others. So you have to recognize it for what it is, and show love anyway.

Most of your focus should be on the child and getting all the help and support you can for them. Get counselling for your child right away. Please do not ignore it or act as if it never happened. It will hurt the child and your family in the future. You yourself should go to counselling to talk out what you are feeling, and allow them to help you help your child. If you are a mother who cannot afford counselling for yourself (as it was for myself), ask to sit in the counselling sessions with your child. A lot of times the counsellor will provide strategies to help both of you in this situation.

Most importantly look to God for your strength, love, patience, and guidance. If this is something you could have prevented in some way, and you see how it has negatively impacted your child, please forgive yourself and ask God to forgive you. Then move on; don't stay in your guilt. It may seem as if God is far away, but He is not. He is right there, so call on Him. God will give you all of the above along with peace to make it through.

You can handle this. Pray and stay strong

Chapter 12:

Looking Ahead and Dealing with the Pain and Loss

As a family, we went to church each Sunday and stayed

active in the things of the Lord. My husband and I started ministers' training classes, and I began leading praise and worship each Sunday and was a part of the intercessory prayer ministry. This is where I learned of the importance of sacrificial worship, which is the worship that God desires. He wants us to worship Him in truth, that means in realness. No phony stuff or doing it because you see others in church but out of depths of your heart. (John 4:24)

My second daughter began her passion by becoming part of the liturgical dance group, and my son started taking drum lessons and joined the youth department and the junior usher board. I also began teaching Sunday school and leading Wednesday prayer calls at noon. I knew there was a call to ministry on my life, so I began to start walking in my call. I began opening up the church services with invocation prayer, and then began to do the ministerial prayer for the pastors or ministers at the ending of the services each Sunday. Even though my home life was challenging, I began to channel that into service to

God and doing the things of God. We became stronger as a family. I became a radical praiser and worshipper. I didn't mind who was watching me; they didn't know my story, and I needed God desperately.

My daughter wasn't easy to parent because she was hurting. She went through a lot of trauma and was angry and needed time to heal. It was extremely hard, but I came to understand. I had to be there for her to listen to and support her and get her all the help I could. This is something that no one gave me. I knew what it felt like to be in her position, so I vowed to myself and God that I would never allow her to suffer alone or in silence. I wanted to give her all the help I could humanly give her and shower her with the love that God could only give. It was definitely not easy, but I was beginning to learn to trust God in this process.

We had a long road ahead of us that included years of trials. God remained faithful to us. We had our good days and our bad days, our ups and downs. She even became physical with me; oh, Lord! I There were days I wanted to put my child in the streets; I felt like I didn't love her. Let me be real with you. She would hit me and try to choke me, and I felt that I didn't love her. She would also tell me she hated she.

The child I birthed out of me? How dare she? How she hurt me, but she was hurting too and did not understand how to speak out her feelings. Because she was hurt it was easier to hurt someone else.

I am not going to tell you that when she said those words I said, "I love you anyway, boo boo." However, I will tell you God is a repairer of relationships even between a parent and child. As parents we also say things we ought not to say to our children, words we need to repent of and say sorry for saying as well. Yes, in my time of hurting, I said some things to my child that hurt her even more, because I was hurt. It didn't make it right.

But when you can come back and repent to God and tell your child at a later time you are sorry, it can really help a lot. This is what I believe helped to repair my relationship with my daughter.

Whoa! Here comes my own guilt, shame, and weight of my past coming back to remind me of the mistakes I made. Even though I prayed and trusted God and tried my best to do the right thing in the eyes of God and my husband and children, I still had not forgiven myself.

I was a victim starting at the age of six years old, and I have always been the victim. To top everything off, I didn't realize I wasn't fully healed from my past hurt, the trauma that happened to me. Even though it happened when I was about ten years old and I was in my thirties, the memories came back fresh right along with the anger and the pain.

This is how you know you have not finished healing. When you talk about the situation (or as in my case, relive it through someone else) and the pain is still excruciating, you are not healed. You have to understand that and allow God to heal you.

It got so bad for me that some days I couldn't interact with anyone. I slept all day, and couldn't face my daughter because even though I was once that abused child, I was hurt and heartbroken, so I began to blame my daughter for the abuse that happened to her. My grandmother taught her from the age of two not to let any man touch her body, and it happened anyway. I couldn't understand how it could have happened when she was taught not to allow this thing to happen. I was taking it personal. I was so torn from my own issues and was somehow projecting all of that onto my child. It was all about me and my hurt.

Some days I couldn't even deal with her because I was so torn from my own issues. I knew I needed counselling but couldn't afford it financially, and I felt I could not pause and work on myself. I had to continue to help her and make it about her. It hurt so much, but God reminded me that she was just a child. I began to remember how I felt when the abuse for me as a child began. I knew it was wrong, and I didn't want to pull my pants down, but I was scared. Scared for my life, scared of what would happen. I didn't want to hurt my aunt. I had no choice but to listen and pull my pants down. So I began to see things through the eyes of my daughter and realized she was also scared and reacted as she was told.

Maybe my decision to not get counselling was not the best one, but it was the best decision I felt was needed at the time. I thank God that He allowed me to see differently in this situation because that is when I could really help her, and as I helped her, I was allowing God to heal me as well. I became a mother she could talk to about anything. I made up in my mind that I would be the parent and the support that I never had. I started going to counselling sessions to talk out my issues and to learn to better help my daughter.

I got deeper into God; I prayed more alone and with my daughter. I deepened my relationship with Jesus because I knew about Him since I was a child, and got to know Him as I got older and understood I needed Him more in my life than I was currently allowing. The way I handled certain things in life was not as good as it should be, and the way I handled God, by not reading His word and talking to Him (praying) as much as I should until issues arose, was the same way. I waited until I was at a low point, then would then lay prostrate and try to seek God's face.

I then realized God is not a puppet, and I couldn't only call on Him when I was going through tough situations or my back was against the wall. I had to call on Him even in the good times. I knew I didn't want to be called on by a friend or family member only when they were in trouble because I would feel like I was being used. So I started to view my relationship with God in that way.

Immediately, I wanted change and repented (asked for God's forgiveness). I also forgave myself for thinking in that selfish way, and then I asked God for His help, His strength, and comfort; basically, I asked for help with everything. I asked Him to help me be there for my daughter and not push her away. I cried out to God. Sometimes I just cried, and I know He heard those prayers, especially on the not so strong days, and I believe He worked on my behalf.

One of the worst feelings in the world is to feel as if nothing but death could be worse than your situation. I was distraught and broken. The very idea my own child was violated made me cringe. I didn't feel I could tell friends or family because of my guilt. How could I have let this happen? I knew the trauma of the situation because I experienced the same as a child.

I felt betrayed by her father, and I hated him. I couldn't understand that after I told him beforehand "watch your daughters" because he had a young adult male family member he didn't know well residing in the home he lived in, how he could have let this happen. He was the one watching the children after school while I was at work. How could this still happen to our child. He neglected to handle his duties as a father, and I was hurt, angry, and felt betrayed. The very same person whom I loved since we were young teenagers, the same guy I dreamed of sharing the future with, no longer existed. Despite ending in divorce, I felt he should have been a part of his daughter's healing process.

To top it off, at the same time, my grandmother was suffering with early symptoms of Alzheimer's Disease, dementia, so her memory wasn't good. Repeating the details of her granddaughter's abuse over and over during each conversation while bathing and cooking her meals for her was not very good for my emotions. All this was done before my work shift started for the day. I was responsible for her, POA (power of attorney) because I was the only person she had. Her two daughters (my mom and aunt) had passed away, and she had a son whom she wasn't close to. She didn't raise him.

My grandmother passed away in 2012; her short sickness and death was a shock and occurred rather quick. I didn't have time to breathe or even stop to figure out how I felt. I considered myself a victim of loss. She was like another mother to me, and I had to prepare emotionally and financially to host a homegoing service for the person I felt would always be around. Two years prior to her death, she took me to the funeral parlor, and I watched her pick out her casket and everything she wanted for her day. It was like she knew she was going soon, but she never told me how real her feeling was. So when your time came, me handling everything the way I knew she wanted, was my way of saying thank you for everything. It allowed me to let her go emotionally and bring myself some peace.

With the feeling of the weight of the world on my shoulders, I felt like any other person would feel when they have gone through so much in life. Yes, I loved the Lord, but there were many days I questioned if He loved me. Sometimes I even felt that God had forgotten me. Everything was going completely opposite of what I had pictured as a good life, and I didn't feel as if I could go on. I had pain; I suffered and had major losses. Still, somehow I found a way to God. I knew in my hurt that I wanted God and felt the urgency.

I would have a vision of a rock, and I had to stay grabbing onto that rock to hold me up from falling into the deep water below. I knew He was there somehow in my life, but honestly, I just didn't realize how close He was to me because of all that I endured in life, and I felt I had much more life to go… My experiences make me think of a man named Job in the Bible who lost everything—all his possessions and loved ones. He even was told to curse God and die. I take my example from Job. He was hit with so much at one time in losses and grief, but he fell to his knees and began to worship God. He loved him so much that he trusted that whatever happened, he trusted God.

So I came to realize the situations were in my life, but I had to view them from a different perspective. Life continued to be a struggle, and I did get weak emotionally and fall from time to time. But in dealing with situations, God was strengthening and maturing me.

Chapter 13:

Too Much Worry, Not Enough Prayer

◇◇◇

However, I became a worrier; I worried about everything.
At first, I didn't realize how bad the worry affected me, but my worship and prayer life began to slip to the point it was neglected, which means I was neglecting God because I allowed all my worries and problems overtake me. I couldn't get up out of bed for work or to simply tend to my children. So I decided to see a doctor.

Immediately, I was put on medication and diagnosed with generalized anxiety disorder; it's a severe anxiety disorder that interferes with daily activities. After I began taking the medication, I started to feel better, but I knew I could not stay on them for life. It was to just get me to a point where I could grab hold of my life again. I was against mental health medication until I had to be the one to use them myself. The anxiety was more manageable with medication, and I was able to pray again. I felt like I was coming out of the big mountain I was under.

Before the medication, I had so much anxiety and built up anger that I began to take it out on people who didn't really deserve it, but

I still lead praise and worship. I still prayed at the pulpit when ask to do so. I still read my Bible sometimes. I still loved the Lord. But I still was broken. No one knew that after I left that pulpit I would go back to living in "hell." How could I do all of that? Because I was anointed; I had issues but I was anointed.

How many pastors and leaders minister from a place of brokenness themselves? Many times you hear people say I am ministering to myself first. We may brush it off or ignore it but it's really true. They are speaking to themselves first. Many people fail to understand that even as leaders in the church, in whatever capacity they may serve in, they are human first. The enemy attacks them also, and even on a deeper level because leaders are on the front line for you.

This is why no one should assume their leader doesn't need prayer or assistance. You should ask how they are doing and pray for them as often as you pray for yourself. Please remember that; pray for your leaders.

So the only way I could have allowed God to continue to heal me and everything about me was to push past every negative emotion and stay in His face in prayer. It was a process. The medication helped, but ultimately, God had to do it for me. The medication was just an avenue that allowed me to stay calmer and clearly think through the next steps.

I really couldn't understand why I was given this life, and I would often ask, *Why me, Lord?* His response was, *Why not you?* I never seemed to get that.

Over the years, His *Why not you?* began to catapult me into my destiny. I learned His answer was really telling me: *I believe in you, and you're strong. I created you and equipped you with everything you need. You just have to hold on and trust Me. No, without me you can't make it. But with me you have everything. So, why not you?*

Glory to God! I knew my struggle wasn't just for me. Because of my own struggle, I would have the answers and the strategy to share with someone else.

Chapter 14:
Road to Recovering It All
◊◊◊

The road didn't get easier; it got much tougher. My mindset had changed, though, and I focused on God because I knew He was my strength. By focusing on God, I was able to view my problems and circumstances differently and then respond differently.

How did you respond? You might ask...

First, I responded by learning and believing who I am in God; I am His daughter, and I prayed consistently asking Him to know more of Him. I started listening to Christian music only, both contemporary and fast-paced songs. (You can listen to whichever you like.) I particularly enjoyed worship tunes.

Replace your secular music with good Christian music. There are hundreds of artists from all cultural backgrounds. I am sure you can find some to purchase or download to your playlist.

I discovered I am a worshipper, and I still love it.

Here is another nugget for you:

If you want God to move in your life, if you want to know your prayers are answered and be favored by God, become a true worshipper! I got the revelation that I needed to be a Judah worshipper and not just a Judas worshipper. A Judah worshipper is a worshipper who worships from the heart, and a Judas worshipper is someone who appears to worship but the heart is not really in it. I understood that God does not want a worshipper like that. He wants a true worshipper, someone that can worship not just with their lips but from their heart. Give all that you can to God. Give of your time and money to those in need. Pray for anyone and everyone: friends, family… I even developed a habit of praying for anyone I feel led to pray for on the street. If I drive past an accident on the road, I pray for the situation, praying for no loss of life. If I see it could be a loss, I pray for the family left behind.

Make sure to give to the church. When you have extra money or time, bless your leader. Those that cover you spiritually. Everything you do, do it unto the Lord.

I look at worshipping God like this: Don't you feel good when people speak highly of you and love you wholeheartedly? Well, how do you think God feels when you are in true worship with Him? He will speak to you in worship. He will change your way of thinking in worship. He will change your situation around in worship. Worship is one of the most powerful weapons you have been given. He created us to worship Him; that's our purpose.

I did what I loved, and I did it each moment I got. I pushed through the moments I didn't feel like worshipping because I felt my strength come from my worship. I walked around my house in prayer in worship. At first, my family would look at me like I was crazy and just sit there, but I didn't care. I needed God! So I continued. Eventually, someone caught on and joined me. My circumstances began to change for the better, I was finally able to breathe. I started to see the son (sun) shining through the clouds.

Each day I continued to feed my spirit with positive uplifting sermons and music. This is how I war through my trials. It worked then, and I'm an even stronger worshipper now.

I learned that helping others, giving in some way—especially out of your own need—is amazing. God honors that. So I became sensitive to God's voice, and whatever God said to do, I would do it. I remember times I would hand people money discreetly in church because I felt they had a need, or I heard God tell me to do so. I would drive on the highway and pay the tolls of people behind me and tell the clerk "Tell them it's paid and Jesus loves them."

The feeling of knowing I was being obedient to God was (and is) priceless. I offered wisdom to anyone I could, and in turn God blessed me. He kept my mind and continued building me up to be strong. I began to turn my victim mindset into a victor. I was no longer was a victim, and I began to kill that victim mindset one demon at a time.

Yes, I said demon. Anything that's not from God is from Satan, the devil. And he assigns his demons to destroy us. Being a victim only acknowledges the victim demon in your life.

Say this following with me; declare it over your life:

> *I am no longer a victim; I am victorious in Jesus's mighty name. No matter what has happened, every demon attached to all the pain and sorrow in my life, every demon who has been assigned to my life to disrupt the plan of God, are now dismissed from my life in Jesus's mighty and holy name!*

Philippians 1:6 says, "Being confident in this, that he who begins a good work in you will carry it on to completion until the day of Christ Jesus."

This scripture verse means that whatever God has started in your life, He will complete. Do you remember when I said you have a purpose? You were actually born with a purpose, and the enemy knows this, so he tries to destroy you so your purpose will not be fulfilled. You see he tried to destroy you from your past trauma, but he didn't. He never wins when he is up against God. God is fighting for you. If He wasn't you probably wouldn't be breathing right now. That's why I mentioned earlier that He is closer to you than you think. He was fighting for you from the very beginning. And you win because of Christ!

You will live and not die to declare the works of the Lord! That means you will live to tell your story and tell of God's goodness and His grace. There is a ministry inside of you that needs to come out. It's the burning desire for something you know is positive. Something that you enjoy doing.

Someone reading may have always seen themselves as a pastor or preacher. You have had dreams at night since you were a little child. Someone else might like liturgical dance; you love music and love to move to the rhythm and beat. What about you who loves to help others? No matter where you are, you always want to help.

Well these are all gifts God has given you, and He gave them to you to use them for His service. Bring others to Him; that's your purpose. You know what God has told you or showed you… It's not too late. You can still do it now; the world is waiting on you. Someone is waiting to hear *your* story.

Do not worry, because worry just places the issues back into your hands to continue to worry about or try to work out. Trying to figure out something that is not yours to figure out in the first place is not good. Every battle you face is not yours; it's the Lords. Keep that in mind.

Second Chronicles 20:15 tells us that: "...for the battle is not yours, it's the Lord's"

A lot of years have gone by since my daughter's abuse and my grandma's passing, and God is still good. My children are well; my oldest daughter is in college and is saved and growing in grace. She ministers to her peers. My other children are saved as well and are growing in God's grace and blossoming into powerful young people of God. I instilled in them from birth to love God with all their heart and soul.

Chapter 15:
Being Free and Staying There
◊◊◊

I am thankful that no matter what happened in life I kept

my children in church and introduced them to Christ. I read somewhere in the Bible that even if the child strays in the wrong direction, if the Word of God is rooted and grounded in them they will find their way back to Him (Prov. 22:6), and because that is the Word of God, I know that His word never fails.

All thanks to God. When the enemy tried all he could, God remained that strong tower for us to continue to stand and fight the battle. Like Job, I have recovered what was lost and more. The relationship between my physical father and myself has been restored; God truly mends what is broken. I became a mentor and spiritual mother to many. I have a good, solid career. God has blessed me to accomplish some lifelong goals. I no longer take anxiety medication; I learned through God how to cope with stress. Step back from the situation and breathe. Seek God because He is the only one who can truly fix things. We may be able to put a Band-Aid on situations or even make it worse.

I decided I didn't want to make messes or just cover up things. I wanted not only put a Band-Aid, but I wanted the wounds and scars to be completely healed. I wanted to get to the root.

Only God can do that. Here's why: when you put a Band-Aid on things, it doesn't heal the wound. It only covers it, and since it's not completely healed, the skin is fragile and can break, and at any time the wound can open up again. Most times, as you probably know, it can open up to be much worse than it was when you first saw it. But getting to the root of the wounds and scars (issues) is like pulling up and out the bad, so the wound doesn't have a chance to reopen or for the bacteria to grow and infect things.

After I allowed God to get to the root of my issues, I started to live better and see real change in myself first. One day, I went to see my doctor; he was impressed with how I was doing, and I was told I no longer needed to take the medication. I didn't stop taking it because I felt I was better though. I waited to be released from the treatment by the doctor. My husband and I are leaders and serve in active roles in the Lord's house. I have remained a worshipper, and God has blessed me because of it.

I began life in hardship and trauma, but that's not where I am now. It is definitely not where I am going because I decided to make Christ the center of all things concerning me.

Don't give up on Him because He has never given up on you. If you do not belong to a church ministry, I encourage you to start going to a church beginning the next worship day. Let me explain: you can worship and praise God at home daily, and you should, but when I say next worship day, I mean either Saturday or Sunday when you can join a church family to corporately worship and praise God together, as well as lift up and encourage each other. Go somewhere that you can hear the Word of God and learn to apply it to your everyday life.

Won't you pray with me?

> *Father, in the name of Jesus, I pray for the individual who is reading this book right now. I ask that You touch the very core of their being. Go deep God…I ask that You heal the core get to the root of their pain, their confusion, their evilness, bitterness, depression, anxiety, sickness, and all that You did not place inside of them. I pray that You uproot it all, leaving nothing behind in the name of Jesus.*
>
> *I come against every demonic assignment that has been particularly assigned to this here Your child. I send that demon back to his place of origin in the mighty name of Jesus. I pray that forgiveness fills their heart right now! I pray that trust in You flows through them right now. Father, ignite a fire in their soul that they cannot control, a fire that will allow them to desire You. Motivate them to run after You. As a deer would pant for water, let their soul be thirsty for You. I pray that You send Your Holy Spirit right now! Awaken the demon slayer in them right now! In Jesus's name. Amen!*

I am lead to speak over your life:

I speak increase to you right now. Increase in your spiritual senses. I pray that from this day forth you will never be the same. Your thinking will change, and the way you handle situations will change for the better. There will be no lack in any area of your life; every need you have is met. I speak that you shall rise like an eagle and go into the enemy's territory in the Spirit and take back all that he has stolen from you. I speak that any dream that God has given to you will come to pass. Your faith in God, your dreams, your goals, your spiritual gifts, are being activated right now, and you will walk toward everything God has for you. Your life purpose will be revealed. I speak that you will get past that divorce, that addiction, that passing away of a loved one, that sexual abuse, verbal abuse, whatever it is that has caused you to become a victim. You will be able to get through it, and not only get through it, you will be able to help someone else along the way. Pay it forward.

The victim slayer has been activated in you! Believe it; receive it, and walk in it.

Don't let anything hold you back from your God-given destiny.

Until we speak again, know that God loves you more than anything in this world. You are special and have been given a purpose.

Pick up and move on. Take the tools you have learned here, and apply them to your own life's situations.

Yes; you're going to make mistakes, just as I have, but the important thing is to realize it was a mistake, ask God for forgiveness and guidance, and then move on. You are no longer a victim of your circumstance. No matter what others may think or say or how they react to the new you, you are a new person. You have been spiritually renewed, and your mindset has changed.

Satan will try to bring back your past to remind and drag you back. You must let him know you that you are not the same. There is nothing you could have ever done that God cannot forgive; He makes you new (2 Cor. 5:17).

You can be free from anything you are doing that may not be godly. Ask God to forgive and help you. Life will not be easy but will be doable. With God you will always have strength and peace, even when you feel you should be upset.

Start off with gaining a relationship with God, so you can know His will for your life. He will equip you spiritually. Remember, any battle you face with Christ, you will win. Trust God because He destroys mountains. You are free from your past, the Bible says wherever God is there is freedom. God resides in you, so you are free! (2 Cor. 3:17).

Conduct yourself always as if God is standing in front of you. Remember, Satan makes you a victim, but God makes you a victor.

Remember to show love in all things. It tells the enemy you are mature in Christ. God is love, and if you don't display love you can't display God. Love was used to save you on Calvary over two thousand years ago.

Trust the process; trust the God Who destroys mountains. Allow Him to work it out for you and trust His timing. He is always on time.

Forgiveness goes a long way. Let it go. Forgive. Do it for you; you deserve to live your best life.

Before reading this book you were a victim, but now God has promoted you. You are now qualified, you have the tools, and I believe have been equipped to begin your journey with your new mindset. So switch your graduation cap tassel to the other side, and walk out into the world as a new person. Your mind is renewed and refreshed. God's got you! Walk in your God-given VICTORY!

God has turned your tragedy into triumph,

your pain into purpose,

and your sorrow into success.

Believe it!

Be blessed!

CPSIA information can be obtained
at www.ICGtesting.com
Printed in the USA
BVHW071732050821
613732BV00003B/364